MW01632174

NEW YEAR - 2023
TO: ELMER HALL
SUNNYBANK INN ...

DITTIES

WHISPERS, SHADOWS, AND SUNSHINE

YOUR ENCOURAGEMENT, YOUR FRIENDSHIP THESE MANY YEARS — BLESSINGS TO ME!

BY

M. J. EBERHART

NIMBLEWILL NOMAD

GOD BLESS YOU,
SUNNY (NIMBLEWILL)

Thirsty Turtle Press™
Evans, Georgia

International Standard Book Number: 978-0-578-26798-2
Library of Congress Control Number: 2022911059

Published in Evans, Georgia, USA, by Thirsty Turtle Press™
4458 Andover Drive, Evans, Georgia 30809

Printed in the USA by Kindle Direct Publishing©
440 Terry Avenue North, Seattle, Washington 98109

Second Edition

Front Cover Artwork by Lena Auxier©
Back Cover Artwork by Lisa Harvey©
Back Cover Medallion by Nathan Wright
Cover Design by Dane Low, Ebook Launch©
Book Scenes Sketched by Lena Auxier©
Edited by Emily Price Soli
Formatted by Andrea Reider

To learn more about *Nimblewill Nomad* and to order *DITTIES* or other books by this author, please visit www.nimblewillnomad.com.

To dear Father and Mother
in loving memory

Elbert Meredith Eberhart, D.O. (1914–1984)
Anna Eberhart, née Johnson (1912–1979)

Publishing a volume of verse is like dropping a rose petal down the Grand Canyon and waiting for the echo.

—Don Marquis

TABLE OF CONTENTS

I. LIFE & INSPIRATION

A Path by the Side of the Road 1
Life's Blessings 2
Ring Out Ye Joyful Bell 3
Path of Faith 4
Finding the Way 5
True Worth 6
Our Maker's Countenance 7
Ma Nature's Splendor 7
No Way Home 8
Reality 10
A Sojourner's Prayer 11
The Pelt and the Feather 12
Prayer for a New Day 13
True Friends 13
Carol's Log Cabin 14
Friends Along the Way 15
Wishing Well 16

A Life of Grace. 17
Ubaldine Dea 18
Going Home. 20
Freedom's Dull Bell. 22
9-11 24
The Lemming. 24
Friars at Graymoor 25
The Enders Family Reunion 26
De Swanee My Home 27
O'er Listening Point 28
Miracles Abound 30
Time for Reward 30
Blessings This Day. 30

II. MYSTERIOUS MEDIUM TIME

The Missing Gene 31
Slow Times. 33
Captor Time. 35
Life's Time Warp. 38
Eternal Mountains. 40
One of These Days 41
A Path Through Time. 43
Loom of Time 46
Time Out. 48

III. THAT FIRE IN OUR GUT

Land of the Free 51
Explorer 52
Mist on the Wind 52
How the West Was Won 53
Just Empties Comin' Back 55
The 100-Mile Wilderness...................... 56
Why Go 57
Newfoundland 58
Zealand Hut 62
Long Gone 62
Chasin' Rainbows 63

IV. HIKING & BACKPACKING

Highlands Journey 65
Spirit of the Mountains........................ 68
The Eastern Continental Trail................ 68
God's Glorious Gift............................ 71
Thru Trails 73
Appalachian Friend............................ 75
No Stroll in the Park 76
Six Lanes Wide 77
The Lone Expedition 78
A Trip on the Ol' AT.......................... 78
Bama Roadwalkin' Friends.................... 79
A Path in the Sky.............................. 80
Pack o' Young Hounds 81
Pennsyltucky Rocks 81

Which Path Indeed 82
The Spirits of Sagamook. 83
Secrets of the Restigouche 84
Ballad of the IAT 86
Cumberland Valley Roadwalk 90
Appalachian Ranger 90
Sprouting Wing 91
The Lord's Mill 91
The House that Jack Built 92
Class of '98 93
Naught but Regret 94

V. NATURE

Ma Nature's Paintbrush 95
Mystical Brotherhood 96
The Long Trail 97
Sweet Shenandoah 98
The Bigelows 98
Little Bigelow 100
A Well-Kept Secret 101
Land of the Seminole 102
Mysterious Pipes of Pan 102
Thunder on the Mountain 103
Little Rocky Row 104
The Last Fall 105
Nocturnal Spell 106

VI. ON THE LIGHTER SIDE

Help Thy Neighbor . . . 107
Good Luck . . . 108
Ol' Staggerin' . . . 110
Truckin' . . . 112
Now Cut That Out . . . 114
Check the Deed . . . 114
Hiker's Scourge . . . 114
Share & Share Alike . . . 115
No Finer Fare . . . 118
Head Phones . . . 118
On Bonefish Sugarloaf . . . 120

LIFE & INSPIRATION

A PATH BY THE SIDE OF THE ROAD (3-01)

Lord, set me a path by the side of the road,
Pray this be part of your plan.
Then heap on the burden and pile on the load,
And I'll trek it the best that I can.

Bless me with patience, touch strength to my back,
Then cut me loose and I'll go.
Just like the burro totin' his pack,
The ox a-plowin' his row.

And once on this journey, a witness for you,
To'rd thy way, the truth, and the light.
Shine forth my countenance, steady and true,
O'er the pathway to goodness and right.

And lest I should falter, and lest I should fail,
Let all who know that I tried.
For I am a bungler, feeble and frail,
When you, dear Lord, I've denied.

So blessed be the day your judgment comes due,
And blessed be thy mercy bestowed.
Oh, blessed be this journey, all praises to you...
O'er this path by the side of the road.

LIFE'S BLESSINGS (7-99)

Don't be dismayed by this world's wealth;
'Haps you've been denied your share.
For the measure used is not always right
In judging what's just and fair.

So go your way, be content each day
With the metes that are handed out.
For you'll find in the end, blessings tend
To banish the sorrow and doubt.

RING OUT YE JOYFUL BELL (9-03)

Ring out, ring out, ye joyful bell,
For long-lost souls forsaken.
For those cast down the road to hell,
Ring back the path they've taken.

Ring out for all with judgment right;
Their courage stands alone.
Our young, our old, who rose to fight,
Ring for their valor shown.

Ring for our sons and daughters, proud,
Who died to keep us free.
For sunrays there behind the cloud,
Ring that we all might see.

Ring for the sadness in this land,
For blessings—quell and heal.
Pray never shall such evil stand,
Ring forth his truth—reveal.

Ahh, yes, ring out, ye joyful bell,
For us whose faith is blind.
Forevermore, pray peace shall dwell.
Ring clear for all mankind.

PATH OF FAITH (11-99)

True happiness is seldom found
Among the polished stone.
For on the path where most have trod,
Scant faith has ever grown.

But should we journey o'er the way
Where less the path is worn,
'Tis there the most-pure radiant light
Brings forth that glorious morn,

Whereon we rise to greet the day
To find our prayers fulfilled.
Here joy and peace fill full our cup
Just like our Father willed.

But, oh, the faith to pass this way,
The path few e'er have known.
For 'til we see God's face have we
Gone long and far...alone.

FINDING THE WAY (10-98/12-99)

It seems God always finds a way
To find a way for me.
His guidance comes through steadfast love;
'Tis there for all to see.

And as I stumble o'er this path,
I need to keep in mind...
That he has cleared a way for me
That faith will help me find.

And as I hike these mountains o'er
And trek the glens between,
The Lord is constant by my side;
His countenance I've seen.

You'll find our footprints in the dust;
There are God's...and mine.
I know at last the worth of me,
The worth of grace, Divine.

Soon will our footprints meld to one,
And at the brink, they'll end.
For there my spirit will be freed
And heavenward I'll wend.

TRUE WORTH (2-98)

There's a Trail,* this grand ol' Florida,
My journ' to find true worth.
'Cross shifting sand, failed mortal plan,
To'rd peace, pure joy...rebirth!

*Florida National Scenic Trail (on the Eastern Continental Trail—Key West to Cap Gaspé/Belle Isle).

OUR MAKER'S COUNTENANCE (5-98)

Our Maker's countenance, 'round,
Seen from these mountains high,
Fills us with peace, profound,
Until the day we die.

MA NATURE'S SPLENDOR (3-05)

Well, I'm trekkin' it hard to'rd that ol' settin' sun.
But it's movin' much faster 'an me.
And the dark's comin' on by the foot and the yard...
My ol' eyes a-squintin' to see.

Yet I hurry my way 'cross the valley beyond,
Through the pass, dim shadows at play.
I glory in thought what this journey has wrought
To delight in this glorious day.

Fir needles my bed, and to pillow my head,
A moss-covered Douglas that's down.
A domain for a king, 'tis a glorious thing,
Ma Nature's splendor—my crown.

NO WAY HOME (12-99)

Those grand old Ozark Highlands,
Fond memories...long ago.
They tug upon my heartstrings
To strum them soft and low.

The melody is pure and sweet,
So gentle on my mind.
I hearken back to home and friends,
A far-off place and time.

I'm there with Mom and Dad again,
With Salle by my side,
With dear friends Don and Larry Jean.
Their love was ne'er denied.

I chose to leave them long ago;
Into the world I went
To seek out fame and fortune's claim,
But 'twas a life ill-spent.

And now this old man has returned,
Filled full with sad regret.
The facts I now must face straight up,
The die's been long cast, set.

For it is true, we can't go home;
We can't go back in time.
Why did I go? Why did I leave
My home, my friends...behind?

So here I stand in my hometown,
An old kid drained of joy,
A-knowin' that I can't go back
To when I was a boy.

I stare into the life I've wrought,
The ending and the start.
And to the "Rock of Ages" now,
I turn with broken heart.

The melody is pure and sweet,
So gentle on my mind.
I hearken back to home and friends,
Another place and time.

Those grand old Ozark Highlands
Await at heaven's door.
'Tis there I'll find my home and friends,
And I will yearn...no more.

REALITY* (7-95)

Life can sure be dandy,
Just like sugar candy.
Beautiful to touch, see...
Yet lacking joy, serenity.

Happy times and suffering,
Plus at least one other thing,
Comes by love to greet me,
Then to test—defeat me.

Now, as to the shambles,
Briars, burs, and brambles.
How do I survive this?
Bourbon, beer—I'll try this.

But...

'Tis a lonely, dead-end out.
To the sky, I scream and shout.
Sets in late—reality!
Lord, forgive...release me.

*After a four-plus-decade marriage—divorce.

A SOJOURNER'S PRAYER (1-00)

Up from the peaceful meadow,
Here drift the Pipes of Pan...
In dream-filled medley mellow,
Unlike the din of man.

Unto me now in calm repose,
They hearken days of yore,
Dear family, friends, and all those
Who've passed to heaven's door.

And so my prayer, a path this day,
From harm and travails be.
Then lead me safely to'rd thy way
'Til pure the light I see.

THE PELT AND THE FEATHER (4-01)

The pelt and the feather,
A Cherokee's love.
The wolf of the nether,
The eagle above.

A life in the high blue,
A life in the glade.
A path to'rd the heart, true,
Glad spirits have made.

Come forth now, the lightning
And thunder and rage.
Sweet death to those fighting,
Sad dawns a new age.

A nation asunder,
Shamed miseries wrought.
Pure beauty and wonder
Through eons is naught.

The pelt and the feather,
A Cherokee's love.
The wolf of the nether,
The eagle above...

PRAYER FOR A NEW DAY (3-02)

Here! A bright new day doth beckon.
Now! A fresh new life begins.
O'er this path I'm soon to reckon,
Lord, cast there my mortal sins.

Let me greet this new day dawning;
Blot all sorrow from my mind.
Free me from all earthly haunting,
Leaving doubt and woe behind.

Halt, dear Lord, this frantic hurry.
Wrest these burdens; rest my soul.
Lift from me all want and worry,
Make me pure, Lord; make me whole.

TRUE FRIENDS (2-98)

True friends are hard to find this day,
Not like in times back when.
So cherish I their love since they
Shan't pass this way...again.

CAROL'S LOG CABIN* (6-98/1-00)

Leaning, yet to time defiant,
Seems it never had a care.
Carol's cabin up the meadow,
Like a loved one standing there.

Oh, what carefree times were spent here.
Might it speak of them this day...
Those to whom it offered shelter,
Since to pass and go their way.

Likened mist cast o'er the Garden
Soon now lifted by the sun,
Family, all—they'll come to linger,
Passing by here one by one.

Bringing memories, cherished ever,
To return unto her care.
Carol's cabin up the meadow,
Like a loved one standing there.

*Inspired by the old log cabin in Burke's Garden, Virginia—and my dear friends, the Chamberlains, who once dwelt there.

FRIENDS ALONG THE WAY (2-01)

Some come into our lives then quickly go;
Some find our hearts to ever stay within.
Either way, their presence strikes a glow,
And we are never quite the same again.

WISHING WELL* (11-05)

Dear friend of mine, long tried and true,
I wish this wishing well for you.
Just pitch a penny in today;
True joy and peace will come your way.

A place of shelter from life's storm
To keep you safe and free from harm.
Then wish your folks and friends be there
With open arms, their loving care.

Wish then the love of all your life,
And she will come to be your wife.
A helpmate, lover, pal, and friend
To hold and keep you 'til the end.

A fruitful life with kids and pets,
No looking back—no last regrets.
And might these dreams (your dreams) come true,
I wish this wishing well...for you.

*To my dear friend, *Sheltowee*—and *Waterfall*, who came to share a fruitful life.

A LIFE OF GRACE* (12-99)

I have a friend who has been dealt
A monumental blow.
For he's not free like you and me;
He can't get up and go.

'Twas on a dark and fateful morn
He most near met his maker.
They pried him from that gruesome scene
To greet the undertaker.

But God was not through with him,
His days here on this earth.
And though he'll never walk again,
My friend has found true worth.

His life he lives full measure,
As good as it can get.
There's not a trace of lingering doubt,
Self-pity, or regret.

You'd think that he'd be bitter with
His quadriplegic life.
But like no man I've ever known,
He's learned to deal with strife.

His faith is solid, firm, and strong,
A glow from deep within.
His countenance from ear to ear...
That old familiar grin!

So when the shuffle's dealt to me
A little out of whack,
I think of this courageous man
To put me back on track.

Oh, what true inspiration!
A blessing he's my friend.
For though his life was over,
He lives his life again.

*Inspired by my dear departed friend, Greg Smith.

UBALDINE DEA (5-00/5-01)

A trail goes past her way,
The IAT.*
And she, one rainswept day,
Befriended me.
Ubaldine Dea.

What joy has come my way,
A mystery.
For miracles, they say,
Are history.
Ubaldine Dea.

A debt I must repay,
Now filled with glee.
I search to find a way
That pleases she.
Ubaldine Dea.

Alas, this dark-gloom day,†
What misery.
I find she's passed away...
To thee.
Ubaldine Dea.

*The International Appalachian Trail (IAT) is a continuous footpath from just outside Baxter State Park, Maine, to Cap Gaspé, Quebec—a distance of some 750 miles. NOTE: The IAT has since been extended north to the island of Newfoundland and across the Atlantic Ocean to Europe.

†I returned one year later bearing gifts for Ubaldine, to find her yard in weeds and the beautiful home that I had remembered in much disrepair. Her neighbors gave me the sad news of her passing.

GOING HOME (10-99)

I've seen the seasons stand their ground,
The flooding rivers stage.
I've seen the mountains blush with fear
Afore the thunderous rage.
I've seen the shadows run their course
Across the meadows green.
I've seen the warm sun cast its spell
With all its magic sheen.
I've seen the morning dew encase
The primal cove and glen.
I've heard the glad voice of the lark,
The beckon of the wren.
I've watched the breeze stir up the trees

To gay, melodic song.
And on that wind, God's gentle hand
To carry me along.
In sun, in rain, storm-laden days—
They're all the same to me.
No doubt, you'll make no sense of it,
A baffling mystery.
But where the mountains part the sky,
Here joy and peace prevail.
The face of God I see...as he
All earthly cares assail.
And by these temples where I rest,
The Lord takes care of me.
There is not one thing that I lack;
I've true serenity.
And so you think that I am poor
And want for sheltered home.
But here in God, I've perfect peace...
For I am not alone.

FREEDOM'S DULL BELL (10-99)

Lord, what's it take? What must we do
To please the powers that be?
How long can we stay on this road?
How long can we stay free?

The smart cats in our government
Can't wait to help us out,
As long as we can make enough
To pay their way about.

Oh, it's so grand that they're in charge
With all their fine advice.
And it's sure good they've duplicated...
All their programs twice!

There'll be a check soon cut for you,
For me 'n all our kin,
As long as we stay true 'n blue
And vote the bastards in.

And up each rung, clear to the top...
A little fatter cat.
They're there to see—Six News, TV;
Don't take my word for that.

Look! There they are, the wise, smart lot
To help us through each day.
For our dependence they must have;
It is the price we pay.

So are we free? Pray, who's in charge?
Who rules our destiny?
How can we longer hope to live...
Independently?

Hypocrisy, democracy,
They cannot coexist.
The way we've gone's entirely wrong...
When will we turn, resist?

Are we not brave Americans,
A fire down deep inside?
What's happened to our dignity?
Oh, where has gone our pride...

9-11 (9-01)

Life lost,
Right bent.
Sorrow tossed,
Purpose sent.
Truth drives,
Love gives.
Joy survives,
Glory lives.

THE LEMMING (1-02)

I'm here among the wretched souls
Whose lives are daily driven...
By all the senseless dead-end goals
That to themselves they've given.

Within their hearts, God's peace and joy
They skillfully suppress.
As on a mission to destroy,
Filled full with deep duress.

They live a life the lemmings live,
Stampeding to'rd the brink.
To never stop, to love, or give—
To never stop and think.

Into this tumult I am cast,
Propelled and dragged along.
While wild-eyed masses thunder past,
A pell-mell, surging throng.

I shout until my voice is hoarse,
“In God’s name, stop and rest!”
But hypnotized, there is no force
To turn them from their quest.

There’s not a one the least aware...
’Til silence comes to set.
Now at the brink, in deep despair,
I’m left with sad regret.

FRIARS AT GRAYMOOR* (7-98)

From this spiritual summit at Graymoor,
O’er the Hudson far away,
See the bright-lit twilight skyline,
The shimmering spires by day.

What is the meaning of all this
Majestic, earthly show?
Only our Savior, the Son of God...
And the Friars at Graymoor know.

*Graymoor, the Holy Mountain—Franciscan Friars of the Atonement, Garrison, New York (on the Appalachian Trail).

THE ENDERS FAMILY REUNION* (11-99/12-01)

A grand old family gatherin'
Of we-uns, 'n you-uns, 'n us-uns.
And mixed right in, a smatterin'
O' friends and kissin' cousins.

And under the spreadin' boxwood,
With green flies buzzin' 'round,
We ate way more than ever we should,
A banquet set for the crown.

The horseshoes a-ringin' 'n clangin',
The joyful laughter of kin,
And sure, some loud haranguin'
Heard over the constant din.

The young-uns a-runnin' 'n rompin',
Folks scoldin' 'em not to shout.
The croquet mallets a-poppin',
The balls a-clickin' about.

I close my eyes and feel it...
The touch of my grandma's hand.
My senses all now reel it.
'Twas a gatherin' oh so grand.

Ahh, yes, what I'd give to relive it,
That glorious grand communion.
For in those hills, my memory dwells...
The Enders Family Reunion.

*Wonderful family, great friends, and grand times in the Pennsylvania Highlands.
Johann Christian Philip Enders (Revolutionary War veteran) and Anna Apolonia Degan Enders, his wife, emigrated to America from Breunigweiler, Palatinate, Germany, arriving in Philadelphia in November of 1764. The Enders likely made acquaintance with and would have known Benjamin Franklin!
The old *Nimblewill* is an eighth-generation Enders descendant in the new world. His lineage: 1-7-1-5-1-10-1-1.

DE SWANEE MY HOME* (2-01)

Dear Mr. Foster,
Would you could have seen
How Nature kept her, blessed her
With beauty pure, serene.

That grand ol' ribber Swanee,
Dere's where de old folks stay.
And with dem folks I'll tarry
When come de judgment day.

De world am sad and dreary,
Eb'rywhere I roam.
But ever in my mem'ry,
De old folks at home.

Yes, down de whole creation,
'Cross rivers and loam,
I searched to blamed tarnation...
No Swanee, my home.

*Variants (dialect and spelling) are pure Foster demotic, taken from his original work "Old Folks at Home." Stephen Collins Foster never saw the Suwannee River, nor did he ever visit Florida. "Old Folks at Home" is (was) Florida's state song.
The intent of this poem is not to *foster* controversy—but rather, to evoke the human experience (the mores) from a vastly different time. The inspiration came while hiking the Florida National Scenic Trail, which follows along the meandering banks of the beautiful Suwannee River for many a mile.

O'ER LISTENING POINT* (2-02)

O'er Listening Point they beckon;
Here haunting pipes enthrall.
Pray tell, perhaps you reckon to
The Piper's far-off call.

Winged on winds that whisper,
Spurred past stampeding steeds,
Pitched low before the vesper,
Hearken...the Piper heeds.

O'er Listening Point they beckon;
Those haunting pipes enthrall.
And now straight forth he reckons
Unto the Piper's call.

To breach the veil, he wanders
To enter eons' race,
Up to the pipes that thunder
To touch the Piper's face.

O'er Listening Point they beckon;
The pipes, our Maker's breath.
And in that final second,
He triumphs...over death.

Ahh!

This very day they beckon!
O'er Listening Point they fall.
We need but pause to listen for
The Piper's far-off call.

*In honor of, and to the memory of, Sigurd F. Olson (1899–1982), distinguished American ecologist and interpreter of wilderness. He was one of the best-loved writers of his time. Sigurd wrote much about the "Pipes," with near reverence.

MIRACLES ABOUND (9-98)

Great miracles abound
Throughout this world of sin.
But we must have an open heart
To take the blessings in.

TIME FOR REWARD (12-98)

There comes a time reward seems due
To those who take a stand.
'Cause from the crew are picked but few
To lead the banner and band.

BLESSINGS THIS DAY (12-98)

As I reflect this day's reward...
The good that's come to me,
I bow my head and thank the Lord
For this grand Odyssey.*

*Odyssey 1998—Eastern Continental Trail.

MYSTERIOUS MEDIUM TIME

THE MISSING GENE (10-99)

It seems that man's incapable
Of comprehending time.
We measure it to go with it,
Yet live in the pure sublime.

We search the sky and ponder, *Why*?
This journ' to'rd eternity.
We know there's time to live...to die,
A time for it all to be.

From where does it come? Where does it go?
It's a total mystery.
Can't the brilliant minds from aged times
Explain it to you and me?

...No!

We're all struck dumb to this medium;
We all have a missing gene.
So along we ride as we bump and glide,
Strapped down in our time machine.

We search ahead with hope, with dread,
What the morrow has in store.
Though we'll never know, straight off we go—
On our journ' to forevermore.

The design of it gives us all a fit,
'Til we ponder the consequence.
Then we travel on to'rd one more dawn,
Though it makes not a whit of sense.

With expectant glee we try to see
Past that shadowy veil adorned.
But the shroud will stay 'til that very day
We rise to our final morn.

Yet as we grope, as we search with hope,
As another step we trod,
Instinctively, we know there'll be...
True peace through the grace of God.

SLOW TIMES (2-01)

Well, forty days 'n forty nights
Ain't really all that long.
But don't ya s'pose it seemed a while
To Noah and his throng!

I'm sure that Jonah had some doubt
About the time it'd been,
'Twixt when he got all swallered up
To pop back out again.

And all them birds in Sing Sing,
The lifers and their lot,
Ne'er had to worry much about
Time bein' in a trot.

Remember old Van Winkle?
When time gave him a Rip,
He shook it off, and up 'n took
Another slumber trip.

Spring's always bullied summer,
While winter badgered fall
To drag along; those times sure seemed
The slowest of them all.

We watched that old gray-bearded gent
A-leanin' on his scythe,
Until that sweet young New Year's babe
Came in to bid him bye.

Well, time's a tough 'n mean ol' crank.
It loves to make us wait.
And don't ya know! The final stall...
At purgatory's gate.

CAPTOR TIME (7-99)

Time is a gift to each and each
That hastens through our life...
Bringing love, contentment, peace,
And a fair-measured bit of strife.

It's provided free to you and me,
Given by God knows who.
And it comes through grace, setting the pace,
Controlling our destiny.

Some fight it hard, by the foot and yard,
Yet along does it choose to go,
As our shoes get worn and our kids get born
And the weeds in our backyards grow.

Explain please, Albert,* this medium
That enslaves us all within.
Why must we march to this cadence drum
To never return again?

Where is the key to that shadowy door,
To our bygones of yesterday?
Where is the path that led from there?
Why can't we go that way?

Why can't we run in childhood fun
With freckles, barefoot, free?
Where went those endless summer days
We romped through carelessly?

What is this time in a bottle
We desperately clutch and hold?
Where went those days called yesterday,
Leaving memories...old?

Why must the seasons come and go,
The years blur by and pass?
What is this thing we're measuring
With sand through an hourglass?

Why does the paint on our dwellings faint?
Why do our teeth fall out?
In order to hear our friends so dear,
Why must they most near shout?

Ahh...yet on we go, hair white as snow,
As our moms and dads bid bye,
To finally turn in despair, and yearn,
And stare to'rd the boundless sky.

But never before have we seen so clear
As our vision begins to dim.
There's order in all, and the orders are:
Report for your interim.

Well...

What was this gift from Captor Time
We've squandered, wasted—gone?
Spent, although we could ill afford,
As we rise to our final dawn.

So find we now in this time-ship line
For that magic carpet flight.
Will the Captor yield as we break its field
And exceed the speed of light?

Since time is grace, as we meld with space,
To enter the realm of Heaven,
We'll finally know, our faith aglow,
The eternal gift that's given.

*Albert Einstein.

LIFE'S TIME WARP (11-99)

Time's such a 'plexing medium;
It's off and then it's on.
At times there seems so much of it,
Yet when we turn...it's gone!

From when I was a little tyke,
I still can hear Mom say:
Now go 'n run, go have your fun,
'Cause you'll grow up someday.

But that day only seemed to come
For all my older brothers.
And aww! Would I sure be like them
If I could have my druthers.

At school, time never seemed to end.
I tried preoccupation,
While both hands on ol' Seth* stood in
Suspended animation.

It seemed to take forever,
Movin' up to seventh grade.
I waited and I waited
While it rained on my parade.

I finally wished away my youth,
Got clear into my teens.
I learned to smoke and kiss the girls
And drive the cool machines.

I finally graduated...
Got a job 'n punched the clock.
And 'long about that time, it seemed,
Time sure began to rock.

For it was there that I got caught
A-sleepin' at the wheel.
The teeter-totter skipped a beat
And time began to reel.

Don't chickens tend to scurry when
Their lazy necks are wrung?
Well, on that roller-coaster ride,
I grabbed a-holt and hung!

All knuckles white, I slammed the bend
And thundered down the track.
I burnt my candle at both ends
And never did look back.

Our kids grew up; life whirred its warp;
Dream-castle goals sped past.
I finally stopped to catch my breath...
And face the final blast.

Then time came to a screechin' halt;
The brakes were firmly set.
The dust was settlin'...yet I knew,
Time weren't through with me yet.

Well...

The teeter-totter now works fine;
I'm rockin' in my chair...ahh!
And time? It's now my long-lost friend,
And neither of us care.

*A Seth Thomas clock.

ETERNAL MOUNTAINS (5-98)

In five hundred million years,
These mountains will be smaller.
Just as five hundred million past,
They were a wee bit taller.

The race of man may race away,
So we'll not know for certain.
But chances are these mounts'll stand
To see the final curtain.

ONE OF THESE DAYS (4-01)

Down through the ages and down through time,
As the mountains wash away.
As the rivers drown to the oceans down,
And the sun warms one more day.

We've all got dreams called "one-of-these-days"
We dearly wish to do.
But ever out of reach, that golden ring
To dreams come true.

There's a journ' that leads to happiness
Past the beaten path we know.
It's on our list called "one-of-these-days,"
But we never stop...to go.

For as we whirl this merry-go-round,
Life's always in the way.
And all our dreams, our "one-of-these-days,"
Get left for another day.

We once were young; our list was short;
There seemed no urgency.
But now we've reached the crossroads
Leading to eternity.

Our list now stretches out the door;
Life's dreams have passed us by.
And with them went our "one-of-these-days"
To greet us by and by.

Yes!

Down through the ages and down through time,
As the mountains wash away,
As the rivers drown to the oceans down,
And the sun warms...one more day.

A PATH THROUGH TIME (9-99)

I see chestnut trees a-growin',
The New River's new course flowin'.
I can see the gray wolf
Huntin' up the ridge.

I see buffalo a-roamin'
And the antelope a-runnin'
Past the ancient mountain's shadow
O'er the plains.

To long patience be you true;
Father Time brings this to you,
From the trove Ma Nature
Clutches to her breast.

Hold your eyes up to your heart,
For it's then that you will start
To see past the shadows cast
Across Time's wall.

You don't need a looking glass
To see into Time's abyss.
There's a vision only Time
(More time) can free.

See on past the bolted door
Into future's well-stocked store.
Here the seasons will reveal
Their brilliant glow.

There's a radiance o'er all;
From the sun it does not fall.
For the speed of light's not
Fast enough for that.

As your heart begins to meld
With the joy these wonders hold,
And you come to marvel
At our Maker's hand.

Don't be timid, don't be shy;
Come along with me...and try
To see past these walls
Thrown up by Father Time.

There's a journey waitin' there;
'Tis a trek I'll gladly share,
As we venture through the future
Past the past.

Oh! The trail is rough and steep,
But no burden-down will keep
Us from climbing up
This skybound path to'rd Time.

As we near our final quest,
As we claim the mountain's crest,
As we stare in awe
At what God has conceived.

On Time's summit we see all,
From life's spring on through life's fall.
There's our past. Look!
There's our future, all revealed.

A 360 revelation,*
Like a glimpse up into heaven.
Here we'll share true joy and peace
'Til time...to fly!

*Inspired by "The Spirits of Sagamook" (9-98).

LOOM OF TIME (11-99)

The tapestry Ma Nature weaves
Upon her loom of time...
Brings lasting grandeur more supreme
Than all of man's design.

And from this warp and woof comes forth
Creations most sublime.
To spin more inspiration than
A poet's clever rhyme.

Where else on earth is man so blessed
With bounty such as this?
To us, like sons and daughters,
She blows her loving kiss.

O'er valleys green with sun-drenched sheen,
Vast skies and oceans blue,
This overflowing treasure trove,
Her gift to me and you.

Wild tumults gray, yet give they way;
Bold circus colors grand...
To play the circuit rider's path
Across this glorious land.

All colors of the rainbow
She blends with earthly tone,
To cast a spell our hearts know well—
Pure beauty, all her own.

The chill, hard cast from autumn's blast,
Stark winter's blinding show,
Spring beauties' dainty, joyful faces
Blend the meadows through.

And on the grand horizon,
There stand the mountains tall,
True temples of God's boundless love...
Triumphant over all!

And so, from sea to shining sea,
Like from far heavens cloven,
O'er all this vast majestic land,
Her tapestry is woven.

A fabric everlasting.
How vain man seems to be,
To think he'll wrack a whit of change
Through all eternity.

Ahh, yes! This grand creation,
Born on the loom of time.
For all to thrill, spellbinding still,
Ma Nature's gift, Divine!

TIME OUT (1-02)

I'm sittin' here on this ol' bench,
The time to while away,
While wifey shops the mall about;
Will take her most the day.

And I been thinkin' how at times
Time sure becomes a drag.
Well, here she comes...to bring me by
Another shopping bag.

I check my watch and shift a bit;
Time's standin' mighty still.
The hour hand sure tends to crawl
When there is time to kill.

But how about when we 'n all
Us boys is havin' fun?
When deal on deal, the shuffle breaks,
And we are on a run!

And what about the times
When we're a-huntin' in the glen?
How long 'til dark? I'll take all bets;
We're sure not waitin' then.

And 'member that old football game?
'Twas tied up, seven–seven.
And we said we'd be home by nine,
But it was pushing 'leven!

Well, boys, it seems there ain't no way;
Time's sure not on our side.
So 'haps we'd best just give 'er sway...
And let the whole thing slide.

THAT FIRE IN OUR GUT

LAND OF THE FREE (12-99)

Here's to all hearts of that cold, lonesome track,
To the life of the wanderlust...free.
To all who have gone and have never come back,
Here's a tribute to you and to me.

With our feet in the dirt, we're the grit of the earth,
Heads a-ridin' the heavens o'erhead.
And they won't find a nickel of value or worth
When our fortunes are tallied and read.

But no richer clan has there ever been known
Since the times of all ruin and wrack,
Than those of us lost to the dust outward blown,
Who have gone...and have never come back.

EXPLORER (7-98)

There is no land discovered
That can't be found anew.
So journey on, intrepid,
Into the hazy blue.

And as you seek your fortune
And near your lifelong quest,
There'll still be countless peaks to climb
Before your final rest.

MIST ON THE WIND (5-98)

Nature's splendor, the great outdoors,
God's glorious wonders to see.
No finer place to enjoy this peace
Than along the old AT.*

A life akin to the mist on the wind,
This, the wanderlust's way.
He'll roam about to his heart's delight,
A calling he must obey.

*The Appalachian National Scenic Trail (AT) is a continuous footpath through the mountains and valleys of fourteen states, from Springer Mountain, Georgia, to Mount Katahdin, Maine—a distance of some 2,190 miles.

HOW THE WEST WAS WON* (12-99)

I yearn for the days of the dust-blown haze
When the West was an infant child,
When the brave, the few, joined lots and threw
Their cares to the wind and the wild.

Thru bone-weary pain, thru mud and rain,
They traveled, a-trustin' God.
As dear-loved kin and many a friend
Were set to rest in the sod.

On to Californ', on to Oregon,
Thru ruts worn weary and long,
'Cross rivers deep, scant rest or sleep,
Passed this destined, fateful throng.

On mules, in prairie schooners,
On buckboards 'n walkin' tall,
Thru Indian lands, their fate in the hands
Of the wagon master's call.

Thru prairie grass, up mountain pass,
They journ'd to'rd the Promised Land.
And along the way, set adrift, they cast
Their past to the shifting sand.

No turning back, thru rut and track,
The wagon trains moved on...
To'rd the western sky, with dream-filled eye,
On the trail to a brand-new dawn.

And to this day do the brave there stay,
Born new from the pioneer age!
A dream fulfilled, as God had willed,
Past the land of the purple sage.

And oh, what I'd give to have journ'd 'n lived
On that trail with those brave and strong.
Now history—times wild and free—
For those days do I yearn and long.

Ahh!

Those were the days, ere time-dim'd haze,
When the West was an infant child,
When the brave, the few, joined lots and threw
Their cares to the wind and the wild.

*I was raised in the Ozark Highlands of Missouri, near that grand old "Big Muddy." A spur, one of many in the overland trails system, once passed by our place. I can remember dad oft showing me, with a faraway glint, an old rock post that was part of a hitching rail along that historic old trail. Ahh! When he would talk about those bygone days, I'd long for them. That was as a child, and in the mind's eye of a child. That childhood memory still resides and is alive and well in the mind's eye of this old man. And here, finally, after all these years, is the humbling proof of it!

JUST EMPTIES COMIN' BACK* (10-17)

I'm hikin' this ol' highway
Right next to the railroad track.
And passin' by this whole long day—
Just empties comin' back.

'Tis time to think about my life;
Sure 'nough it's out of whack!
While yet another train goes by—
Just empties comin' back.

As go these trains, so goes my life;
I've never had the knack
To string together piddlin' more—
Just empties comin' back...

*Inspiration for this ditty came during my Historic Route 66 trek—while hiking many a mile "Right next the railroad track." I was also inspired by the thought-provoking poem "Empties Coming Back" by Angelo de Ponciano.

THE 100-MILE WILDERNESS (10-98)

A trail through Maine's north wilderness,
Past bogs and ponds of blue,
Beckons the restless wanderlust
Down deep in me and you.

So off in the swirling mist we go
With our boots and raingear on,
While friends at home and folks we love
Try figurin' what went wrong.

But we'll rove these woods and mountainsides,
A-waitin' that by-and-by,
A perfect dawn...when packs take wing
And the treadway climbs the sky.

WHY GO (1-01)

It's the people, the places,
The pain and the trials.
It's the joy and the blessings
That come with the miles.

It's a calling gone out
To a fortunate few...
To wander the fringes
Of God's hazy blue.

NEWFOUNDLAND (9-01)

Back in the haunts where shadows, long cast,
Chase the faraway corners of time,
Search there through the tomes of centuries past
For a glimmer of reason or rhyme.

Great Norsemen in longboats set out to sea,
Sails furled to the rush and the roar,
Each one of them bent with a yearn to be free—
None daring a look to the shore.

Sailed forth those great warriors on uncharted wind
To'rd lands where the sun seldom sets,
Thence tacking to port for a southerly bend,
Set they all, nary one with regrets.

Pitched up o'er the depths in the frightening grips,
Through a tumult of violence and rage,
Came men steeled in armor aligning their ships
Into fear, their foe to engage.

True venturers, they, to the ends of the earth
Where told fierce dragons kept wait,
Testing their mettle, their valor, their worth,
Their destiny sealing their fate.

Yet forth from the shadows did images form
Thru the brine-crested, shimmering hue,
And out of the gale and the teeth of the storm,
The sails of their ships came to view.

Time-shrouded in mystery, Vinland of old—
Thought only a scheme of the mind—
Defiantly stand where Vikings so bold
Carved marks in the land of the wine.

Oh, hearken that time—to have lived, to have sailed!
As only Leif Erikson knew...
A journ' throughout history all thought had failed,
Set his flag 'cross the surf-driven blue.

Came they to newfound land, these venturers bold,
To lands set adrift in the sky,
Where glacier-torn mountains so ancient and old
Inspired both their mind and their eye.

This place? L'Anse aux Meadows, here puzzled about,
Lie fragments of history's truth.
And so to a world filled with wonder and doubt,
Revealed! America's youth.

So come all ye doubters to Vinland's glad days,
To these meadows on Newfoundland's shore,
And witness, a-mingling the centuries' gray haze,
America's past...evermore!

Ahh, yet comes another, his story to tell,
O'er hills set apart from the sea...
From lands of a nation where millions now dwell
To these hallows where man was set free.

So stand, ye true helmsmen; set wind to your sail,
Outbound on a journey anew,
And test your true mettle and fearing to fail
And quit dreaming the doing...and do.

ZEALAND HUT (7-98)

We're at the hut on Zealand,
And from this vantage watch
The wind drive out the storm clouds
Down in Carrigan Notch.

The sun is dancing 'long the ridge
In splashing yellow hue.
This show? A reckless beckoning
A-callin' me and you.

LONG GONE (3-00)

The long-distance hiker, a breed set apart
From the likes of the usual pack.
A-hoistin' his gear, he knows in his heart
He's gone...long 'fore he'll be back.

CHASIN' RAINBOWS (6-85)

There's a trail way up yonder I'm fixin' to hike;
It has no beginning or end.
But a-waitin' that journey ol' AT...'n I'll be
Chasin' rainbows 'round the next bend.

HIKING & BACKPACKING

HIGHLANDS JOURNEY (10-01)

The mountains are temples for seekers of truth,
Old testaments chiseled in stone.
Here seraphs come winging from fountains of youth,
And we are no longer alone.

The toil of the climb, heart-pounding, the drum,
A realm of the here and the now...
Old memories past, sunrises to come,
We falter to cradle our brow.

We cling to a dream; we struggle and grope;
We worry and trouble the trail.
While all the time doubting, yet hoping on hope,
While all the time fearing to fail.

Comes now the true journey, a proving of mind—
The days pass so fleetingly fast.
What joy to see clearly where once we were blind;
Our prayers are all answered at last.

How can there be sorrowful pain and war?
A quandary to you and to me.
For up here with Nature, no window or door,
From trouble we're sheltered and free.

The highlands, a sanctity welcoming all,
The bosom of God's holy grace,
Where gathereth creatures both mighty and small
In Nature's enfolding embrace.

For here nearest heaven, the days are so sweet—
The essence of peacefulness, joy.
And all the true goodness we ever could meet,
Our senses are keen to employ.

On rolling green meadows where breezes drop in,
We linger to dance in the grass.
And here we set down all our burden from sin
To the trail...'neath our feet as we pass.

Glad waterfalls leap to the heavens, exclaim,
Free at last from the clutches of earth.
Cast out our heartbreak, sorrow, and shame.
Rejoicing a life of rebirth.

Oh, what is this tugging we feel in our heart
That's calling so clear and so loud?
And what is this instinct that sets us apart
From the masses, the rest of the crowd?

We might as well ask for the secret to time
And solve then the mystery of space,
For man can find neither the riddle nor rhyme
To puzzle the pieces in place.

So journ' we the highlands, near heaven on earth,
Truth-testing our mettle and mind—
A pathway to wisdom, right judgment, and worth
That's eluded near all of mankind.

SPIRIT OF THE MOUNTAINS (9-00)

The mountains stand majestically
For all of man's enjoyment.
And each the clan, engaged are we,
Full-time, in that employment.

We trek the good trek past these hills
In search for answers to...
A journ' of faith our Father wills
O'er pathways right and true.

Set to this task, we faithful home,
To'rd lasting, blessed peace;
Unto that light, no more to roam,
'Til God our souls release.

THE EASTERN CONTINENTAL TRAIL* (7-01)

A magic trail that wends its way
Along the mountain crest,
From high the cliffs of Cap Gaspé
On down to old Key West.

I set upon this path alone,
A journ' to find true worth.
And as the way to me was shown,
Came peace, pure joy, rebirth.

For to me as I walked the land
Sprang forth a boundless love.
From unclenched fist, the open hand
Revealed the turtledove.

The way of God is not of man;
At least this much is true.
His path is sure a finer plan
He's set for me and you.

With laden pack all shouldered up,
I entered on that way,
As Nature's nectar from her cup
Sustained me day to day.

O'er mountain high, thru valley deep,
The trail continued on.
And as in dream-filled, endless sleep,
The days have come and gone.

This path, like life, a burdened path
Filled full with strife and care.
The Devil heaped a ton of wrath,
But God was there to spare.

My life, this trail, are trailing out.
The days turn short...I long.
But homing now, in gladness shout,
Filled full with joyful song.

With final steps, I wend my way—
Ten million, more or less.
And I, naysayer, now must say...
To miracles confess.

I thank you, Lord, for all your grace,
For all your blessings, too.
This trail's indeed a holy place;
It's brought me home...to you.

Ahh!

A magic trail that wends its way
Along the mountain crest,
From high the cliffs of Cap Gaspé...
To end in old Key West.

*The Eastern Continental Trail (ECT) is a footpath through the mountains and valleys of sixteen states and two Canadian provinces, from the southernmost point on the eastern North American continent at Key West, Florida, to the Cliffs of Forillon at Cap Gaspé, Quebec, where the mountains plunge to the sea—a distance of some 4,800 miles.

GOD'S GLORIOUS GIFT (8-99)

Nature's beauty and splendor,
God's glorious gift to me...
Now from a start, with an open heart,
As I look, I truly see.

Somewhere I read what Benton* said,
How our vision and mind disconnect.
We look, but see just a mystery
That's baffling, incorrect.

David† started this whole thing off,
Down on his hands and knees,
As he gazed in awe through Walden's hall
From the dust to the sky-brushed trees.

The lands we love are touched from above
With the grace of our Maker's hand.
From sea to shining sea, you'll find
Nowhere on earth as grand.

So come with me to our primal grove
Where the waters and mountains meet,
And lift your eyes to'rd the canopied skies,
Cathedrals in grand retreat.

Come sleep once more on the forested floor
As galaxies whirl above...
Then climb at dawn to'rd the peaks beyond,
Temples of God's pure love.

So don't dismay this troubling day;
You'll prove, the challenge met.
As friends naysay and loved ones pray,
You'll find there's no regret.

Just journey on, intrepid one;
Come join this Odyssey.‡
And we'll fix our head t'what Benton said:
"To see what we truly see."

*Emile Benton MacKaye (1879–1975): The father of the Appalachian National Scenic Trail, a fourteen-state National Park greenway extending from Maine to Georgia. "Let us tarry awhile 'til we see the things we look upon."
†Henry David Thoreau (1817–1862): "...There I can walk, and recover the lost child that I am without any ringing of a bell..."
‡The Odyssey of '98, Sunny *Nimblewill Nomad* Eberhart (1938–): A journey of 298 days and 4,400 miles on the Eastern Continental Trail.

THRU TRAILS (8-99)

Friends long past,
Like dusty gems.
Memories whorl;*
I think of them.

All compass points,
From there they came.
Then on those winds,
They passed again.

We hiked together,
Hearts of pride,
Far o'er these ancient
Mountainsides.

AT was home,
Our quiet space.
We sought and found
Elusive peace.

A rag-tag family
That we were,
We came together
From afar.

Each one was cut
From special stuff.
Each loved...but I loved
Not enough.

Hoist then their packs,
Sky-dark good-byes,
No words to comfort
Rain-filled eyes.

Then off they faded,
Past the mist.
More hearts to weigh
My lonesome list.

Oh friends, dear friends,
Why did you go?
Time seemed so short...
I miss you so.

You passed like God's
Sun-lifted dew.
Memories whorl;
I think of you.

Dear friends long past,
Heart-giving, true,
Memories whorl;
I think...of you.

*As the perfect whorl of the sweet-petaled rose so whirls...

APPALACHIAN FRIEND (12-99)

A friend is here and waits for you,
The quiet, patient one.
Until all things with more to-do
In life are finally done.

'Tis then that you will realize
The path you should have trod.
And in this friend most learned, wise,
You'll search the face of God.

Now on this path you chance to seek,
For you have learned through life...
From those you love, who oft did speak,
The way to break from strife.

Who is this friend? The trail toward
Yourself! Free conscience know.
O'er mount and mead and brook to ford,
This journ' you'll finally go.

And searching now, your life near spent,
In Nature's bosom find
Your answered prayer, aft' deep repent,
True joy and peace of mind.

NO STROLL IN THE PARK (4-98)

Folks, this ain't no stroll in the park,
And sure 'tis not a picknickin' lark.
'Cause gettin' out trekkin' this ol' AT,
There's a price to pay—believe you me!

SIX LANES WIDE (3-98)

The trail leaves Springer Mountain
Six lanes wide, deep trodden.
But narrower it will become
Before I reach Katahdin.

THE LONE EXPEDITION (5-98)

The Lone Expedition* adrift in the clouds,
The Odyssey† lost in the glade.
Half a century apart, the intrepid move on,
Joined through time by spring's gay parade.

*The Lone Expedition—Earl *Crazy One* Shaffer's '48 AT thru-hike.

†The Odyssey—Sunny *Nimblewill Nomad* Eberhart's '98 AT thru-hike.

A TRIP ON THE OL' AT (6-98)

Friendship and frolic, pain and fear,
In the wilderness, footloose and free,
Stir them all up and brim-fill your cup
For a trip on the ol' AT.

BAMA ROADWALKIN' FRIENDS (3-98)

Let me explain about the folks
That live down here in Bama.
They're still into the family thing;
They take care of their momma.

They are a quiet peaceful lot
And tend to mind their business.
There's sure no animosity,
Just plenty of forgiveness.

They'll work all day for little pay,
But when it's time to quit,
They'll go the bayous and the bay
To fish a little bit.

I spent most near a month down here,
Walkin' across their land.
And all the folks I chanced to meet
Held out a helpin' hand.

So though this was a roadwalk,
Three hundred fifty-three,
It was indeed the coolest part
Of this grand Odyssey.*

*The Odyssey of '98 took me by the winding byways and dusty old backroads of southern Alabama...and the beautiful people living there.

A PATH IN THE SKY* (4-02)

The paths are all open; the heaven's aglow;
And I am awaiting this journey to go.
You've been here beside me, both steadfast and true,
To help and to guide me, all life's ventures through.

Since early in childhood, I've known of the need
To reach beyond malice and hatred and greed.
I've failed at each challenge, each labor, each trial.
I've failed at each step, Lord; I've missed by a mile.

The paths of this life, I've sure beaten down,
In search of your light, rare jewels in your crown.
A life of transgression, a life filled with sin—
It's time for confession; Lord, cleanse me within.

Then lift and release me; it's time that I fly.
Oh, Lord, I beseech thee, a path in the sky.
Your presence is in me; it's chiseled in stone.
Forgive me, Lord...take me, Lord...
Make me your own.

*In memory of my friend Earl Shaffer.

PACK O' YOUNG HOUNDS* (6-98)

This pack o' young hounds can burn the trail;
They been taught to bear the torch.
While this old dog, tucked-in tail,
Watches quietly from the porch.

Skitz, Fletch, Hopalong, U-Turn, Flint, and *Birch* (all 4-mph power hikers).

PENNSYLTUCKY ROCKS (7-98)

The rocks of ol' Blue Mountain
Strike brutal and relentless.
Lord, on your help we're countin',
As we are near defenseless...

These ribs of Pennsyltucky
Form backbones sheer and rough,
And we are downright lucky
To make it through this stuff.

WHICH PATH INDEED (7-98)

The trail goes up and over,
Seldom leads us down.
But at most treadway junctions,
There's a shortcut into town.

Now Warren* has been known to ask,
Which path will you choose?
The answer: One small glimpse at life...
Who'll win, and who will lose.

*Warren Doyle, Jr.—Backpacker and raconteur extraordinaire. Founder of the Appalachian Long Distance Hikers Association (ALDHA).

THE SPIRITS OF SAGAMOOK (9-98)

The summit of ol' Sagamook
Isn't all that high.
But as I climb, I pass right through
The bottom of the sky.

From here, I turn to look and gaze
Into the wild blue yonder,
And try and try as best I can
To comprehend its wonder.

Now from this lofty firmament,
I let my spirit soar
To mingle with the spirits of
Great Nations gone before.

And as I part this sanctity,
A bit of me will stay
To rest in God's eternal peace,
That's present here...today.

*On September 26, 1998, trail day 253 and trail mile 3,783, I climbed Sagamook—a lesser-known mountain along the International Appalachian Trail in Mount Carleton Provincial Park, New Brunswick Province. There, on that day, occurred part of what shaped the Odyssey of '98 into the miracle it has become. I share this experience in my book *Ten Million Steps*, where you can read the accounting of it.

SECRETS OF THE RESTIGOUCHE (10-98)

The secrets of the Restigouche
Are only known to me:
The first to hike this river trail
Along the IAT.

All through these mountains, there is cut
A canyon long and deep.
And to its flank rush joyful brooks
From gulches rough and steep.

And o'er this all, the trail is laid—
Not for the faint of heart—
Built by a chap they call Maurice,
A classic work of art.

If in you there's some mountain goat,
Will serve you well, indeed.
Surefootedness on mountain walls,
A skill that you will need.

'Twill take you days to hike this thru;
The miles you need not rush,
For it will take the strongest man
And turn his limbs to mush.

So if you've got the yearn and bent,
I'd recommend to you
To come and see what I have seen
And plan to tough it through.

And now I bid thee, Restigouche,
Enchanted land, farewell!
If you would know its secrets...come,
For I will never tell.

BALLAD OF THE IAT (10-98)

The Appalachian Mountains
Don't end in northern Maine.
For as you tack a northeast course,
They re-emerge again.

They climb to stand triumphant
Through New Brunswick and Quebec,
And o'er them wends the IAT:
A dreamer's perfect trek.

No mountains stand the likes of these
Down in the forty-eight.
A wild yet stately majesty
You'll find they radiate.

Here, rugged mountain men do speak
Strange words in softest tones.
While in them born a hard tough style,
No meanness in their bones.

Bring me a man who makes friends fast,
And I will bet you this:
Give me a day in Canada,
And I'll have a longer list!

Down in the States' vast wilderness,
You thought you'd seen it all.
In Canada, it doesn't end
'Til past horizon's wall.

You've hiked by ponds and lakes and brooks,
Fell captive to their spell...
But here, somehow, your heart turns warm
In their forbidding chill.

Up through the Whites and Presidents,
You touched the alpine zone.
But in the Chic-Chocs, you're above the trees
For miles...alone.

On earth we search for perfect peace;
It is our lifelong quest.
Up here, you'll feel God's presence 'round
And in you as you rest.

For God's hands hold these mountains up,
His tabernacles high.
You'll never feel more close to him
Until you cross the sky.

So come see the rivers Restigouche,
The lovely Madeleine,
The Tobique and the Upsalquitch,
And all 'em in between.

They'll fill your heart with playful glee;
Their happy songs you'll hear.
Come seek their gladness in the fall,
That magic time of year.

You've seen the bear, the moose, the deer,
And if that pleases you,
Come climb Mont Albert's* tundra high
And see the caribou.

For here you're nearing Santa's land
With reindeer roaming free.
You'll hike a wonderland of snow:
A Christmas fantasy.

And if scaling mountains to the blue
You'd rate a perfect day,
Then come traverse the Chic-Choc Range
And climb Jacques Cartier.*

You'll stand spellbound while 'round you'll see
Mont Albert's skyland tundra,
And to the north, clear to the sea,
More of God's boundless wonder.

Katahdin is the grand finale
On the old AT.
But you've not seen the final act
Until you're at the sea.

For to'rd the cliffs of Cap Gaspé,
The Appalachians wend.
And there you'll scale your final mount,
Pass round the final bend.

And so your trek's not over;
You'll need to follow me...
And hike these northern, far-off lands
Along the IAT.

*French pronunciations (approx.): Al-bear; Cart-e-a.

CUMBERLAND VALLEY ROADWALK (7-98)

Come look o'er this Eden, the Cumberland;
Come walk through this valley of time.
On a crisp, clear Sunday morning,
Hear the peal of the church bell's chime.

Through the waving fields of golden grain,
By the springs of Conodoguinet,
O'er byways, past boroughs, and quaint old farms,
'Tis a journey you won't forget.

APPALACHIAN RANGER (9-98)

If you'd like to try and hike
The Appalachian Chain,
Your trek won't start on Springer,
Nor will it end in Maine.

On down to where they say "y'all"
Is where you'll need to go.
Then hike on o'er Katahdin
Into the driving snow.

SPROUTING WING (6-98)

An earthbound mystery,
The strangest thing.
Backpack up, the closer we...
To sprouting wing.

THE LORD'S MILL (6-98)

From the constant grind of this old AT
Comes the grist to try a man's soul.
But from the Lord's mill
Grinds the strength and the will
To carry us on to our goal.

THE HOUSE THAT JACK BUILT* (5-98)

You squirrel in the food
And load your pack
To lug it along
O'er the boundless track.

The more you haul,
The more you eat...
To get the juice
To'rd your screamin' feet.

But the more you tote,
The worse you wilt,
To finally toss the house
(off your back)
That Jack built.

*A spoof inspired by "This Is the House that Jack Built," an old English nursery rhyme.

CLASS OF '98 (9-98)

We all left Springer 'long 'bout spring
To hike this famous trail.
Now here we are, what's left of us,
The few that didn't fail.

The end's in sight, our final quest;
We'll all soon graduate.
'Tis bittersweet; good-bye, dear friends—
The Class of '98.

Ahh, and...

With tears in my eyes, and lingering good-byes,
And a slap on the back or two,
In my journal I wrote this short entry note:
My (thru) hike o'er the AT...is through.

NAUGHT BUT REGRET (7-86)

When it's dismal and dreary,
When you feel there's no hope,
When your heart's filled with naught but regret...
May your thoughts all be heady,
Your pack featherlight,
And the trail six lanes wide when it's wet.

NATURE

MA NATURE'S PAINTBRUSH (10-98)

Ma Nature's got her paintbrush out,
Brushin' o'er the green.
From her palette, every hue
To brighten up the scene.

In red and orange and yellow,
She paints so brilliantly.
And there, a touch of umber—
She threw that in for me.

Now, what's all this excitement?
It happens every fall.
It's nothing but a rerun,
In case you don't recall.

Well, we've seen the works of masters
Hanging in our galleries.
But none can match Ma Nature's hand
When she paints autumn's trees.

Ahh, 'tis a magic time of year,
A spell cast over all.
For all the seasons we hold dear,
The best by far...is fall.

MYSTICAL BROTHERHOOD (1-00)

'Twas once a mystical brotherhood
In the depths of the forest wild...
A code unspoken, yet understood,
Where each saw the other as child.

And so this spiritual fellowship—
Unshakable, firm, and strong—
Shaped all things within its grip
Throughout the forest throng.

In glad refrain, they'd greet the day,
Hearkening Nature's will,
Content in their work and in their play;
To her call, to each task—fulfill!

'Twas not the least disharmony
'Twixt all this sociable clan.
Least that's the way it used to be
'Fore the meddling of (master?) man.

And so came he to this magic place,
No matter he shouldn't or should.
Now all that's left is sad disgrace
In that mystical brotherhood.

THE LONG TRAIL* (8-98)

There's a mystic shade of green
Sets the rainbow's show to want,
Seen o'er these verdant mountains
From the Long Trail in Vermont.

*The name Vermont is derived from the French words *verd mont* (green mountain), so named by Samuel de Champlain in 1647.

SWEET SHENANDOAH (6-86)

You can keep your wine
And your bourbon and your beer.
Just hang on to your scotch and gin
And other forms of cheer.

Don't offer me no sody pop,
No coffee or no tea,
For I am high on Shenandoah's...
Pure sweet majesty.

THE BIGELOWS (9-98)

The Bigelows of western Maine
Are something to behold.
'Twill take a chapter in my book,
A story yet untold.

I'll write about the mountains lush
With birch and fir and spruce.
You'll read about the porcupine,
The beaver, and the moose.

I'll write so vivid, you will hear
The calling of the loon...
Across the silent, high-held ponds,
Pure diamonds in the moon.

You'll understand why Percival*
And Myron† loved this place.
I'll paint in words a picture
Of its majesty and grace.

And when you go to close the book,
And put it on the shelf...

BEWARE!

'Twill haunt you 'til you've seen
The Bigelows...yourself.

*Percival Proctor Baxter (1876–1969): A native and former governor of Maine. He gave the land now known as Baxter State Park, location of Mt. Katahdin, to the people of Maine. Percival loved the Bigelows.

†Myron Haliburton Avery (1899–1952): A resident of Maine all his life. Myron almost single-handedly built the Appalachian Trail. He, too, loved the Bigelows. A 4,000-footer in the Bigelow Range is named in his honor.

LITTLE BIGELOW (10-98)

I stand on Little Bigelow
In all its majesty,
While all around, vast wilderness
Is all that I can see.

Once lived a man who loved this more
Than anyone I know.
Tears cloud my view of Avery Peak
From Little Bigelow.

A WELL-KEPT SECRET (6-99)

A well-kept secret known to few
Where folks say "sir" and "ma'am"
Are the ancient Appalachians
Down south in Alabam'.

Straight from the start, they were set apart
From the rest of their far-flung kin.
And throughout time in this southern clime,
They never quite fit in.

Yet here they sit to the spite of it
Majestic, proud, and free.
And I would rate my hike* here
A great, grand part of this Odyssey.

You can roam all o'er that famous trail
From Baxter to Springer Mount.
But you'll wind up short and to no avail
When it's down to the final count.

So come feast your eyes where these mountains rise,
Where this magic all began:
A well-kept secret known to few...
Down south in Alabam'.

*The Pinhoti Trail.

LAND OF THE SEMINOLE (1-98)

From dark forests deep
Where cypress weep
And black tannic rivers roll,
Always has been,
'Twill always be,
Land of the Seminole.

MYSTERIOUS PIPES OF PAN (6-98)

Far o'er the peaks of Otter,
Across the meadows of Dan,
Hark! From afar they beckon...
The mysterious Pipes of Pan.

THUNDER ON THE MOUNTAIN (5-01)

The mountain fills with thunder;
It's hollow and it's wild.
Now full with fright and wonder,
I cower like a child.

The cymbals are a-crashin'
'Cross Devil's avenue.
Comes now an urgent passion
To right my life anew.

I've lived a world of pleasure,
With not a care to show.
To never fret the measure,
The price for sinning so.

There's thunder on the mountain,
A wicked, timeless space.
The Devil's now a-countin'
His joy in my disgrace.

The lightning flashes white, 'round;
It brings me to my knees.
While in its grip my thoughts drown;
My mortal senses freeze.

The spell leaves me suspended,
To hover in its glow.
And when it's finally ended,
I've little life to show.

The mountain's filled with thunder;
It's hollow and it's wild.
And I no more shall wander;
My sins...now reconciled.

LITTLE ROCKY ROW (6-98)

Gazing in wonder down on the James
From Little Rocky Row,
The manes of a million galloping steeds
Blaze white in the noonday glow.

Such beauty and splendor viewed from above;
From above, 'tis a gift to me.
A sign of our Maker's steadfast love
Through time, 'til eternity.

THE LAST FALL (10-00)

Fall leaves are falling in showers,
Sun-drenched in crimson and gold.
And here in these lofty towers,
A ritual both solemn and old.

A mood swing from joy to sadness,
Another autumn is cast.
Amid all this splendor and gladness,
I ponder, *'Haps this be my last.*

NOCTURNAL SPELL (7-98)

Stars delight, fireflies bright,
Dim shadows from the moon.
Then comes dawn to capture night
And ends the spell...too soon.

ON THE LIGHTER SIDE

HELP THY NEIGHBOR (10-99)

A hard knock came upon my door;
'Twas then most nearly three.
So I got dressed and stumbled down
To see who it might be.
And as I opened up the door
To stare into the night,
A drunk in sodden stupor stood...
Sure gave me quite a fright.

I managed, "Man, what do you want?"
"I need a puth," he said.
That ticked me off; I slammed the door
And climbed back up to bed.
While nodding off, dear wifey said,
"What was that all about?"
And when I told her the ordeal,
She cussed me near clean out!

I pleaded, “Dear, the man was drunk;
He didn’t know his name.”
She said, “That doesn’t matter;
Should’ve helped him just the same.”
By then the clock was striking four,
And I got dressed again
To stumble down the stairs once more...
And aid this stranded friend.

As I stared out into the gloom,
He was nowhere about.
“Do you still need a push out there?”
I cupped my hands to shout.
In slurred reply I heard him cry,
“Oh yesh, come puth me pwease!”
And so I groped to find him...
On the swing down in the trees.

GOOD LUCK* (11-99)

Good Luck was my three-legged hound;
He hobbled his whole life through.
No finer friend could a man ever have;
He was faithful, kind, and true.

Good Luck ne'er had the least good luck,
But he sure brought loads to me.
Was sheer, pure joy just havin' him 'round;
'Twas plain for all to see.

Well, the poor lad had the mange real bad,
Shed most near all his hair.
His face was scarred from fightin' hard,
And he had but part-a one ear.

Ol' Good Luck's luck oft' ran amuck.
And one gray wintry morn,
I fired to'rd a hare in the thicket there...
And that's how his tail got shorn.

His face was a droop; he stood in a stoop,
But he hardly complained a bit.
We'd load in the truck, ol' me 'n Good Luck,
And there by my side he'd sit.

He sure would miss me when I'd go;
He'd mutter the whole day long.
But he'd come a-draggin', stub a-waggin'
Each day when I got home.

I dearly miss that kind old friend;
His big ol' heart jus' quit.
I'll never get over him bein' gone;
I'll never get used to it.

For Good Luck was my three-legged hound;
He hobbled his whole life through.
But no finer friend could a man ever have;
He was faithful, kind, and true.

*Inspired by Spike, a dear old family friend—faithful, kind, and true!

OL' STAGGERIN'* (10-99)

Ol' Staggerin' 'n me was
Headin' up the trail one day,
Across the mesa lookin' for
The signs of J-Bar stray.

Now Staggerin' don't mind too keen;
He's sorta Devil driven,
And soon he sets us straight upon
A right-short trail to Heaven!

So there we was, jest hangin' out,
Ol' Staggerin' 'n me,
To cogitate the coming fate
Most like to set us free.

Ol' Staggerin' would soon cut loose
And we'd accelerate,
To poke them doggies straight along
To'rd purgatory's gate!

'Twas then I whipped my hogleg out
And shot that rattler dead.
Ol' Staggerin' bowed up his neck
And heaved his mangy head.

I never rid a ride like that;
Shore seemed my judgment day,
But odds be with us drovers,
Games of chance jest seems our way.

So...off into the sunset
One more tall tale done told,
Rides *Nomad* on Ol' Staggerin'
From bygone days of old.

*Inspired by the humorous cowboy artwork created by my friend, Nate Owens, in a piece for Leanin' Tree entitled "Lookin' Up."

TRUCKIN' (11-98)

Backpackin's just like truckin'—
Gotta figure gross and tare.
For whatcha pack upon your back
Won't soon be comfy there.

So scrute your lading, net it out;
And sure to your dismay,
You'll find how little you can haul
With joy from day to day.

And as you're truckin' up the trail,
Reality sets in.
'Tis then you'll rip into your pack
And cast out all that sin.

A sigh! The time of truth is nigh,
Great fear and trepidation,
As you search for some answers to
Your hopeless situation.

Ahh!

Now choose 'twixt what you think you want
And what you truly need—
A humbling revelation,
Casting out material greed!

Let's look...what are these niceties?
My lord! Four extra pair.
And what are all these other things
You've squirreled away in here?

"Enough, enough! What is this stuff?"
So sez yourself to you.
"Without that fadget or this snix,
I really can make do."

Yes! Get relief from all that grief;
'Twill set you footloose...free!
And you'll go forth with no remorse
As joyful as can be.

And so, to sing as birds on wing,
Mere feathers on their back,
Just 'liminate that dreadful weight
You're haulin' in your pack.

NOW CUT THAT OUT (6-86)

Well, I cut the last switchback, skid-tumbled and fell,
And got wracked like I knowed that I would...
But in four thousand miles, I saved eighty-six feet,
And that really made me feel good!

CHECK THE DEED (5-86)

The shelters belong to the mice family;
We hikers, intruders of late.
When they kick and cuss and come after us...
Wonder what they'll be usin' fer bait?

HIKER'S SCOURGE (10-98)

When your friends are hikin' slow
And movin' sorta funny,
'Tis monkeybutt they're sufferin',
I'll bet you any money.

Oh, what a dreadful malady,
A scourge upon our masses.
Raspberries are for eatin',
Not for 'round our cheeks and arses!

A little chafing we'll endure;
We'll tuff it with the best.
But monkeybutt will bust your nut,
A brutal acid test.

Should this remain a chronic pain,
There is a cure, you know:
Toss out your toidy paper
And go straight to melted snow.

So don't dismay; soon comes the day
You'll feel both spry and fit,
Though monkeybutt will wrench your gut
Each time you think of it.

SHARE & SHARE ALIKE* (2-00)

Ol' Gram and Gramps to Burger King
To have their strength restored,
One order was the only thing
That they could both afford.

The kiddie menu, burger, fries—
The grand old couple took
The little bag that Grampy buys
O'er to the corner nook.

And from his pocket Grandpa got
His little pocketknife,
Dividing there the meager lot,
The half to give his wife.

And Grandma, counting out each fry,
To Grandpa, half she gives...
While folks around begin to sigh
At how this couple lives.

Now from a table 'cross the way,
A younger couple there:
"Can we another meal to pay
So you won't have to share?"

The old man smiles a tooth-filled smile,
Their kindness to decline.
"We always shared, the whole long while;
We always done just fine."

Now not a dry eye in the place,
A lady came and stood:
"Please let us help you just in case;
It'd do us all some good."

Most shyly then Grandma replied,
"You all are very kind.
We're always by each other's side...
So don't you never mind."

Grandpa, his half-a burger et,
Has finished with his fries.
The saddened lot do now regret
And finally realize...

That Grandma hasn't touched a bite.
The folks all wonder...why?
"Perhaps we've filled her full of fright;
She seems so very shy."

Now up and comes this little lad
O'er to the old folks' table,
And with a face so mournful sad...
"Grandma, you look so feeble!

Why won't you eat your little meal?"
"Well, now that Grandpa's done,
I get the teeth; that's been the deal,
So don't you fret, my son."

*Inspired by an old tale spun so well by my good friend Chuck Parham, since departed.

NO FINER FARE (10-99)

Two robins were a-baskin' in the sun,
When 'long comes momma cat and little one.
And little one sez, "Ma, what do I see?"
And Ma sez, "Son, it looks like lunch to me!"
And as they sized the situation up,
'Twas then ma cat and kitten chose to sup.
Two robins chose to lounge without a care,
So that day, Baskin-Robbins® was the fare!

Now whatcha think of this hilarity?
Aren't words sometimes as funny as can be?
Well, life can sure be dull from time to time,
And so this old bard's job...some playful rhyme.

HEAD PHONES (10-99)

Telephone implants—a marvelous thing!
Even friends 'round you cannot hear it ring.
The transmitter's wedged in your palate bone,
The receiver stuck down your auricular zone.

It's a minor procedure and surgically safe;
The CPT code is 5-7-0h-8.
Surgeons just call it a phone prosthetic,
With all the fees covered by Major Medic.

A blink of the eye and you've got a line out,
And you dial the number by pinching your snout.
It is a quite simple, ingenious thing,
For your party is there on the very first ring!

The taller you are, the reception—more clear,
As the antenna's hooked to a fob in your ear.
You put 'em on hold with a jerk of the neck
And nod your head forward to hit disconnect.

But now I must tell you...there's one thing to know:
These telephone antics create quite a show.
And friends will soon question 'bout your sanity,
'Cause how could they know that you're talkin'...to me?!

ON BONEFISH SUGARLOAF (12-98)

The folks in the Keys, quite interestingly,
Sip their beer through a straw.
They scorch their fish four shades of black,
Yet eat their shellfish...raw.

Indeed, they're as kind as any you'll find
'Long main street US of A.
They'll stop 'n help us strangers along,
Even give us the time a-day.

The weather down here...hey, fine all year,
'Cept for the hurricane.
But the locals'll hunker and ride 'er out
Through the roar and the walls a-rain.

No finer place will you find on the face
Of this earth for your holiday.
The weather's warm, and the local charm
Boasts a paradise for play.

So come on down...jus' lounge 'round
And let ol' Sol kick in.
'Twill warm your heart, and your bones'll start
To feel like they'll work again.

Yeah! Folks done questioned my sanity,
But the smartest thing I done
Was to save the last of this Odyssey*
For the Keys and the tropical sun.

*The Odyssey of '98 started and ended in Florida—298 days, 4,400 miles o'er the Eastern Continental Trail.

The loss of quiet in our lives is one of the great tragedies of civilization, and to have known even for a moment the silence of the wilderness is one of our most precious memories.

—Sigurd Olson

Made in the USA
Monee, IL
29 December 2022

b01edc2c-2cce-4037-be80-2a221899446dR01